NINJA WOODFIRE ELECTRIC BBQ GRILL &

SMOKER COOKBOOK FOR BEGINNERS

2000 Days of Delicious Recipes for Every Outdoor
Cooking Adventure and Smoking Techniques for
Beginners

TYLER .A. MCDANIEL

CHAPTER THREE: BEGINNER-FRIENDLY BURGERS 39

CHAPTER FOUR: GRILLED VEGETABLES FOR STARTERS 54

CHAPTER 5: SMOKED PORK RIBS 69

CHAPTER FIVE: SMOKED SALMON 84

CHAPTER SIX: FLAVORFUL SMOKED VEGETABLES................................99

CHAPTER SEVEN: NEXT-LEVEL TECHNIQUES FOR BACKYARD GREATNESS 114

INTRODUCTION

Welcome to Flavor Country: Your All-Access Pass to Woodfire Grilling Greatness

Have you recently wandered into the promised land of mouthwatering, woodfired cuisine thanks to the trailblazing Ninja Woodfire Grill? Then get ready to become lord of the backyard flames. This standout smart grill doesn't just sizzle and smoke—it paves a path to transcendent cooking that will awe your inner circle. But mastery doesn't happen overnight. Like Yoda harnessing the Force, you must first understand the basics before unleashing your grill's full potential.

That's why we've created this comprehensive, first-of-its-kind guidebook aimed at transforming weekend warrior rookies into seasoned grill masters. Consider this your personal roadmap to woodfire excellence. We'll navigate you through every corner of capability – from grill setup, to smokehouse techniques, to chef-driven tips for incredible flavors – all field tested specifically for the revolutionary Ninja Grill so you can skip the frustrating trial-and-error phase.

What exactly will vault your cooking skills to the next level while unlocking show-stopping creations to make guests beg for your secret? An entire arsenal of prowess awaits within these information-packed pages. We'll provide easy-to-execute methods for perfecting authentic woodfired classics like succulent ribs, smoky whole chickens and tender low 'n slow pulled pork so incredibly delicious you'd swear it came from a championship pitmaster's secret stash.

And it only gets better from there. We'll school you on how to leverage both direct and indirect grilling zones to achieve picture-perfect sear marks on sizzling steaks, vibrant grilled veggies bursting with flavor, and choices like juicy wood-kissed salmon and cedar plank scallops that sound fancy but come together lickety-split. Even showstopping centerpiece feasts like brick chicken and spice-crusted beef tenderloin seamlessly transition from intimidating to extraordinary thanks to the Ninja's trailblazing versatility. Oh, and let's not forget about the dreamy homemade artisan pizzas emerging from the dedicated pizza oven attachment to elicit genuine food envy from your social circle! Let the mouthwatering journey begin!

Grilling and Smoking Basics

While the Ninja Woodfire Grill offers trailblazing features, grilling and smoking rely on time-tested techniques. Let's explore the fundamentals.

Grilling Directly Over an Open Flame

This classic live-fire grilling method involves cooking foods directly above the heat source. Dropping a thick, juicy steak over a hot grill is a perfect way to achieve a flavorful sear while imparting that quintessential charbroiled taste. Grilling over direct heat is ideal for meats, fish, veggies, and more.

Grilling Indirectly Away From an Open Flame

Indirect grilling comes into play when dealing with larger, thicker cuts of meat—like a whole chicken or rack of ribs—that require longer cook times. With indirect grilling, the heat source sits to the side while food cooks gently over the entire grill surface. This allows food to cook evenly without risk of burning.

Smoking Low and Slow

The alchemy of smoking rests entirely on low, consistent heat paired with fragrant woodsmoke. Your Ninja Woodfire Grill brilliantly merges an electric heat source with real wood chunks for authentic smoked flavor. Loading up the chamber with woodchunks (we'll get to wood selection later) and keeping temperatures between 225-275°F is the golden rule for smoking. At this low range, meats tenderize while absorbing deep smoky richness.

Helpful Tools and Accessories

Take your culinary skills to the next level with this arsenal of essential grilling and smoking tools:

Tongs & Spatulas – These extensions of your hands flip, grab, and move food safely. Go for long handles and scalloped edges.

Instant-Read Thermometer – Monitoring temperature is crucial. An instant-read thermometer gives precise readings in seconds flat.

Oven Mitts & Gloves – Protect your hands from searing-hot grates and chambers. Choose long, insulated mitts that allow dexterity.

Stainless Steel Scrubbers – Useful for clearing grill grates of residues without damaging the protective seasoning.

Disposable Aluminum Pans - Perfect vessels for holding marinades, bbq sauces, and excess juices.

Fuel & Woodchunks – Stock up on charcoal briquettes or hardwood chunks like hickory, maple, cherry or mesquite to infuse rich flavor.

Grill Brush and Cleaners - After each cookout, give your grill a thorough scrub-down to prevent future flareups.

Heavy Duty Foil – Useful for quick cleanup. Tent foil over food for easy transport.

Grilling and Smoking Techniques

Grilling Perfection: Mastering Direct & Indirect Heat

One of the Ninja Woodfire Grill's prime functions is classic grilling over an open flame. Let's break down best practices.

Direct Heat Grilling

Searing steaks, chops, fish fillets, shrimp, firm vegetables and more over direct heat keeps foods moist while adding delicious charred bits. Use direct heat for foods that cook quickly at higher temperatures. Preheat your grill fully before adding food.

Helpful tips for direct heat grilling success:

- Pat foods dry before grilling

- Oil the hot grates right before adding food (use high smoke point oil)

- Don't peek/flip too often

- Move food around heat zones (hotter/cooler areas)

Indirect Heat Grilling

This gentler approach prevents larger cuts like roasts, whole chickens or ribs from charring on the outside before the inside finishes cooking. Set up a two-zone fire, with no flames under the food and burner/coals lit on one or both sides.

Helpful tips for indirect heat grilling success:

- Maintain an even, consistent temp between 300-375°F

- Keep the lid closed as much as possible

- Add smoking woodchunks for extra flavor

- Use a thermometer to monitor doneness

Smoking: Infusing Foods with Delicious Woodfired Flavors

For smoky goodness, the Ninja Woodfire Grill's dedicated smoking chamber truly sets it apart from the competition. Follow these guidelines for mouthwatering results:

Choosing Your Wood

Hardwoods like hickory, maple and mesquite impart slightly different flavor nuances. Hickory leans hearty, maple offers sweetness, while mesquite brings an earthy edge. Experiment to discover your favorites.

Setting Up for Smoking Success

1) Soak woodchunks in water 30 minutes (allows cleaner burn).
2) Load soaked chunks into the chamber's fuel bed.
3) Keep temps between 225-275°F.
4) Place protein and veggies in smoking chamber; maintain temp and smoke levels.
5) Check doneness with thermometers. Allow 1-2 hours smoking per pound of meat

Infusing Smoke Flavors

The key is going low and slow in the smoking chamber to give the woodsmoke time to penetrate. During longer smokes, add a few soaked woodchunks if smoke levels diminish. The result? Deliciously smoky flavors!

Innovative & Unique Recipe Ideas

While classic BBQ flavors never disappoint, the Ninja Woodfire's exceptional capabilities open up a world of culinary possibilities. Take your grilling game to the next level with these creative recipes:

Woodfired Carnitas Street Tacos

Transform standard pulled pork into splendid Mexican carnitas, kissed with hickory smoke and crisped to perfection...then pile it sky-high on little street taco tortillas. Ole!

Grilled Maple Dijon Salmon

This sweet and tangy salmon underscores why the Ninja can excel at both grilling and smoking. Hot-grill the maple-glazed fillets over direct heat before transferring them to the smoking chamber for a touch of hickory-scented sweetness.

Smoked Duck Breast with Cherry Glaze

Duck might sound intimidating but the Ninja woodfire allows you to smoke and render its fatty skin for crispy texture. After a couple hours of smoking, lacquer the duck with a glistening cherry sauce for dynamic flavors.

Pizza Potluck Party

The Ninja Pizza Oven attachment transforms your grill into a powerful pizza oven. Use both direct and indirect zones to bake up a bounty of personalized pizzas for a fun, memorable potluck event. Guests can pick their own epic toppings while the crispy, smokey, melty magic unfolds!

Maintaining Your Grill for Peak Performance

Your Ninja Woodfire Grill & Smoker merits proper care and maintenance to keep it firing on all cylinders for years of trusty service. Follow these top tips:

1. Empty ash bin regularly. Excess ash can impact airflow.

2. Use protective covers when storing. Investing $50 now prevents expensive replacements later.

3. Clean regularly. Wipe down exterior stainless steel surfaces. Use non-abrasive cleaners only.

4. Deep clean the interior 2-3 times per grilling season. Scrub grates, clear grease, clean out the smoking chamber and ash bin.

5. Watch for spider nests! Cobwebs can lead to fire flare ups. Vacuum out any webs.

6. Perform protective seasonal maintenance. Weatherproof cords/connections. Clean fan areas.

7. Check wood chunk box gaskets/seals for wear at least twice per season.

We hope this detailed introduction has inspired you to fire up your innovative Ninja Woodfire Grill & Smoker! From mastering basic grilling techniques to exploring inventive recipes to maintaining your appliance, you now have the knowledge to unleash your grill's full potential. Just imagine the magical moments, mouthwatering meals, and memories this do-it-all grill will help create this season and for years to come. Now grab those tongs and get grilling, smoking...and most importantly, enjoying time together around this sensational grill with family and friends!

15

CHAPTER 1: GETTING STARTED -

PREPARING FOR CULINARY GREATNESS

Welcome to the flavor-filled world of Ninja Woodfire Electric BBQ Grill & Smoker cooking! In this chapter, we'll comprehensively guide you through the foundational steps for grill setup, safety precautions, control mastery, cleaning procedures, and preventative maintenance. Follow our lead, and you'll quickly progress from grilling novice to backyard BBQ pro. Let's ignite your Ninja journey!

Initial Setup for Smoking & Grilling Success

Cooking transcendent meals begins with proper grill assembly and location. These starting blocks set the stage for smoky deliciousness.

Assembling your Trailblazing Grill

Your innovative Ninja Woodfire Grill arrives with detailed graphics for streamlined assembly. AllTools and hardware are included along with step-by-step instructions. Assembly time averages 60-90 minutes, sometimes quicker with an extra set of hands. The process includes:

• Constructing the stand and attaching the support brackets

• Mounting the hopper assembly

• Inserting the fuel and smoker trays

• Attaching the cooking chambers

• Installing handles and hooks

• Adding thermometers/dampers

During assembly, heed all safety precautions like wearing gloves when handling sheet metal components. Take care to not pinch wires or tubing to prevent gas/electricity issues. Lastly, ensure all screws and fasteners are tightly secured before use.

Strategic Grill Placement

The ideal site for your Ninja Woodfire Grill is:

• Outdoors ONLY (Dangerous carbon monoxide is produced indoors)

• 10-15 feet from siding, plants, etc.

• Protected from wind

• On a non-combustible surface like concrete, gravel, or bricks

• Near a grounded electrical outlet with sufficient amperage

• Under an outdoor kitchen hood vent (recommended)

• Away from sprinklers

• Visible when cooking (Don't leave unattended)

Position the grill accordingly as an essential safety step before lighting your inaugural fire.

Control Mastery: Understanding Your Grill's Brain

The control panel is essentially your grill's brain, powering ignition, regulating temps, adjusting smoke levels, and monitoring precision cooking. Become one with your grill's gray matter!

Button Functions

The LED-backlit control panel allows you to deftly:

• Ignite the grill via push-button electric start

• Choose between 8 temperature presets (Smoke, 250°F, 325°F, 400°F, 500°F, Air Crisp, High Sear, Self Clean)

• Toggle between cook modes: Smoke, Roast, Grill, Air Crisp, Bake

• Operate interior grill lights and chamber fans

• Adjust time and probe thermometer alarms

• Power down completely

Monitoring Progress

In addition to pre-programmed buttons, your Ninja Grill provides real-time feedback through:

• LED screens displaying set-point and actual temps

• Thermometer ports for digital meat probes

• Glass windows to visually assess doneness

• Smoke level windows to gauge thickness

By keeping an eye on these cues, you'll become a true grillmaster.

Essential Cleaning & Preventative Care

Before lighting up the grill, establish proper maintenance habits. Just 10 extra minutes after each use keeps your Ninja sparkling for the long run.

Post-Cook Cleaning Best Practices

After each grilling or smoking session:

- Brush/scrape residual ashes from grate interiors
- Remove grease drippings from drip trays
- Empty ash bin as needed
- Replace foil on grease catch pans
- Wipe down exteriors with stainless steel cleaner
- Clean grates thoroughly with grill brush

Between-Use Protective Steps

To safeguard your investment during storage periods:

- Install weatherproof grill cover
- Disconnect and store electric cords safely
- Check/address small repairs promptly
- Keep grilling area clear of flammable debris

By embedding these post-cook cleans and between-use best practices into your grilling routine now, you'll avoid headaches later and can focus purely on the food!

Grilling Mastery - Essential Techniques for Woodfired Greatness

It's time to elevate your culinary prowess with the exceptional grilling capabilities of your Ninja Woodfire Grill. Whether you're a seasoned pro or backyard rookie, this chapter unlocks the essential skills for grilling nirvana. Let's explore the art of direct vs. indirect grilling, temperature control, proper searing and more. With these techniques under your belt, you'll be wowing guests with restaurant-caliber cuisine lickety-split!

Direct Grilling: The Classic Live Fire Method

Harnessing direct heat the time-honored way, with food positioned right above the heat source, remains a foundational grilling technique for good reason. That signature sear and char infuses flavor while the quick, hot temperatures lock in moisture. Follow these best practices for direct grilling success:

Prime Applications

Typical foods well-suited for direct, high-heat grilling include:

- Steaks, chops and kebobs
- Boneless chicken pieces
- Seafood like shrimp, scallops and fish fillets
- Firm vegetables like asparagus, peppers, onions
- Fruit slices
- Breads and pizzas

These quick-cooking items shine over a hot, direct flame. Shoot for temps between 450-550°F.

Strategic Setup Steps

Follow this checklist to guarantee direct grilling excellence:

- Preheat 5-10 minutes

- Clean/oil grates

- Pat food dry

- Arrange coals for even heat

- Use tongs for easy maneuvering

- Resist poking/flipping excessively

- Heat can vary, so watch closely

- Remove food once ideal doneness/char is achieved

Mastering these fundamentals lets you concentrate on flavor crafting through marinades, rubs and more.

Indirect Grilling: Two-Zone Cooking for Large Cuts

While the direct approach offers live-fire fun, indirect grilling shines when dealing with thicker foods requiring gentler heat over longer periods. Here's how it works:

Process Explained

Indirect grilling involves zero flames directly underneath the food. Instead, all heat/coals are shunted to one or both outer edges of the grill. Food sits over the relatively cooler center zone, with the lid closed. The indirect radiant heat slowly roasts meats while infusing moisture. It's a winning technique for:

- Whole chickens, turkeys

- Racks of ribs

- Tri tips, shoulder roasts

- Briskets, pork butts

- Cornish hens, duck

• Thick chops (1.5 inches+)

For true smoked flavor, add woodchunks to the heat zone. Shoot for 275-350°F.

Nailing the Setup

Perfectly configuring your grill for indirect heat means:

• Ignite charcoal on ONE side only

• Pour water in unused side's charcoal tray

• Close lid after placing food in center zone

• Add soaked woodchunks to fiery side as needed

• Rotate food if browning unevenly

• Use thermometers to gauge doneness

Temperature Control for Precision

Whether direct or indirect grilling, monitoring temperatures enables you to utterly nail the perfect doneness from rare to well-done.

Thermometer Basics

Two essential thermometers for the griller's arsenal:

Instant-Read Thermometer – Insert probe end into thickest meat sections at end of cook time to gauge doneness ranging from 120°F (rare) up to 165°F (well-done).

Ambient Grill Thermometer – Monitors overall interior temp gauges. Clip external probe to grate, keeping reading visible through window.

Mastering Heat Zones

Your Ninja Woodfire Grill offers exceptional temperature control via multiple discrete heating zones. Maximize this flexibility by:

- Searing foods initially over highest zone setting

- Shifting items needing gentler heat to a lower temp zone

- Closely monitoring zone heat levels and food doneness with thermometers

- Adjusting zone heat up/down as needed for desired cook results

Searing for Superior Flavor & Texture

That crave-able dark brown crust with a crunch seals in moisture while adding tremendous flavor depth. Let's decode the art of searing:

Chemistry of the Sear

Two chemical processes create optimal sear magic:

- Maillard Reaction – Sugars/amino acids in meats brown.

- Caramelization – Natural sugars brown in veggies/fruits.

Best Practices for Next-Level Searing:

- Pat food extremely dry before searing

- Allow grill to preheat fully, 550°F+

- Use tongs to place food gently on grates

- Resist poking or moving food initially

As you move from grilling newbie to pro by honing these essential skills, remember—practice makes perfect. So fire up the grill, get hands-on experience under your belt, and wow your inner circle with sizzling summertime creations. The power of woodfired greatness awaits!

CHAPTER TWO: CLASSIC GRILLED CHICKEN

Lemon Herb Grilled Chicken

Prep: 15 mins | Cook: 20 mins | Serves: 4

Ingredients:

- 600g chicken breasts
- 2 lemons, juiced and zested
- 3 tbsp olive oil
- 2 cloves garlic, minced
- 1 tsp dried thyme
- Salt and pepper to taste

Instructions:

1. In a bowl, mix lemon juice, zest, olive oil, minced garlic, thyme, salt, and pepper.
2. Marinate chicken in the mixture for at least 30 mins.
3. Preheat Ninja Woodfire Electric BBQ Grill & Smoker.
4. Grill chicken for 8-10 mins per side until golden and cooked through.
5. Serve hot, garnished with fresh herbs.

Tips: Add extra lemon zest for a burst of citrus freshness.

Nutrition Info: Calories: 280 | Fat: 12g | Carbs: 3g | Protein: 35g

Garlic Rosemary Marinated Chicken

Prep: 10 mins | Cook: 25 mins | Serves: 4

Ingredients:

- 800g chicken thighs
- 4 cloves garlic, minced
- 2 tbsp fresh rosemary, chopped
- 3 tbsp olive oil
- Salt and black pepper to taste

Instructions:

1. Combine minced garlic, rosemary, olive oil, salt, and pepper in a bowl.
2. Rub the mixture over chicken thighs and let it marinate for 20 mins.
3. Preheat the grill to medium-high heat.
4. Grill chicken for 10-12 mins per side until internal temperature reaches 75°C.
5. Rest for 5 mins before serving.

Tip: Serve with a side of roasted garlic mashed potatoes.

Nutrition Info: Calories: 320 | Fat: 18g | Carbs: 2g | Protein: 38g

Prep: 12 mins | Cook: 18 mins | Serves: 4

Ingredients:

- 700g chicken wings
- 4 tbsp Dijon mustard
- 3 tbsp honey
- 2 tbsp soy sauce
- 1 tsp paprika
- Salt and pepper to taste
-

Instructions:

1. Mix Dijon mustard, honey, soy sauce, paprika, salt, and pepper in a bowl.
2. Toss chicken wings in the mixture and let it marinate for 15 mins.
3. Preheat the Ninja Woodfire Electric BBQ Grill & Smoker.
4. Grill wings for 8-10 mins per side until crispy and golden.
5. Drizzle extra glaze before serving.

Tip: Garnish with chopped chives for a pop of color.

Nutrition Info: Calories: 250 | Fat: 10g | Carbs: 15g | Protein: 28g

Prep: 15 mins | Cook: 20 mins | Serves: 4

Ingredients:

- 750g chicken drumsticks
- 1/2 cup soy sauce
- 3 tbsp honey
- 2 tbsp rice vinegar
- 2 cloves garlic, minced
- 1 tsp ginger, grated

Instructions:

1. Combine soy sauce, honey, rice vinegar, minced garlic, and grated ginger.
2. Marinate chicken drumsticks for 30 mins.
3. Preheat the grill to medium heat.
4. Grill for 10-12 mins per side, basting with marinade.
5. Serve with sesame seeds and chopped green onions.

Tip: Cook until the internal temperature reaches 74°C for juicy drumsticks.

Nutrition Info: Calories: 290 | Fat: 12g | Carbs: 20g | Protein: 26g

Prep: 20 mins | Cook: 15 mins | Serves: 4

Ingredients:

- 500g chicken breast, cubed
- 2 tsp smoked paprika
- 1 tsp cayenne pepper
- 3 tbsp olive oil
- Salt and pepper to taste

Instructions:

1. In a bowl, mix cubed chicken, smoked paprika, cayenne pepper, olive oil, salt, and pepper.
2. Thread onto skewers and let it marinate for 15 mins.
3. Preheat the Ninja Woodfire Electric BBQ Grill & Smoker.
4. Grill skewers for 6-8 mins per side until charred and cooked through.
5. Serve with a cool yogurt dip.

Tip: Soak skewers in water for 30 mins before threading to prevent burning.

Nutrition Info: Calories: 240 | Fat: 10g | Carbs: 5g | Protein: 30g

Prep: 10 mins | Cook: 20 mins | Serves: 4

Ingredients:

- 600g chicken thighs
- 3 tbsp olive oil
- 2 tsp dried oregano
- 1 tsp dried thyme
- Zest and juice of 1 lemon
- Salt and black pepper to taste

Instructions:

1. Mix olive oil, dried oregano, dried thyme, lemon zest, lemon juice, salt, and pepper.
2. Marinate chicken thighs for 15 mins.
3. Preheat the grill to medium-high heat.
4. Grill for 10-12 mins per side until golden and cooked through.
5. Sprinkle extra herbs before serving.

Tip: Serve with a side of Greek salad for a complete meal.

Nutrition Info: Calories: 280 | Fat: 15g | Carbs: 2g | Protein: 34g

Maple Dijon BBQ Chicken

Prep: 12 mins | Cook: 18 mins | Serves: 4

Ingredients:

- 700g chicken wings
- 4 tbsp maple syrup
- 3 tbsp Dijon mustard
- 2 tbsp soy sauce
- 1 tsp smoked paprika
- Salt and pepper to taste

Instructions:

1. Mix maple syrup, Dijon mustard, soy sauce, smoked paprika, salt, and pepper.
2. Toss chicken wings in the mixture and marinate for 15 mins.
3. Preheat the Ninja Woodfire Electric BBQ Grill & Smoker.
4. Grill wings for 8-10 mins per side until caramelized and sticky.
5. Brush with extra sauce before serving.

Tip: Use a meat thermometer to ensure wings reach an internal temperature of 75°C.

Nutrition Info: Calories: 260 | Fat: 11g | Carbs: 20g | Protein: 25g

Prep: 20 mins | Cook: 15 mins | Serves: 4

Ingredients:

- 800g chicken thighs
- 1 cup plain yogurt
- 2 tbsp tandoori spice mix
- 2 tbsp lemon juice
- 2 cloves garlic, minced
- Salt and black pepper to taste

Instructions:

1. In a bowl, mix yogurt, tandoori spice mix, lemon juice, minced garlic, salt, and pepper.
2. Marinate chicken thighs for 30 mins.
3. Preheat the grill to medium-high heat.
4. Grill for 7-8 mins per side until charred and fully cooked.
5. Garnish with fresh coriander before serving.

Tip: Serve with naan bread and cucumber raita.

Nutrition Info: Calories: 310 | Fat: 15g | Carbs: 6g | Protein: 38g

Prep: 15 mins | Cook: 20 mins | Serves: 4

Ingredients:

- 700g chicken breasts
- 2 tbsp Cajun seasoning
- 3 tbsp olive oil
- 2 tbsp lemon juice
- 1 tsp garlic powder
- Salt and pepper to taste

Instructions:

1. Mix Cajun seasoning, olive oil, lemon juice, garlic powder, salt, and pepper.
2. Marinate chicken breasts for 20 mins.
3. Preheat the Ninja Woodfire Electric BBQ Grill & Smoker.
4. Grill for 10-12 mins per side until cooked through.
5. Sprinkle extra Cajun seasoning before serving.

Tip: Serve on a bed of rice for a complete meal.

Nutrition Info: Calories: 260 | Fat: 13g | Carbs: 2g | Protein: 32g

Orange Ginger Glazed Chicken

Prep: 15 mins | Cook: 18 mins | Serves: 4

Ingredients:

- 600g chicken wings
- 1/2 cup orange marmalade
- 2 tbsp soy sauce
- 1 tbsp fresh ginger, grated
- 1 tsp garlic powder
- Salt and pepper to taste

Instructions:

1. Mix orange marmalade, soy sauce, grated ginger, garlic powder, salt, and pepper.
2. Toss chicken wings in the mixture and marinate for 15 mins.
3. Preheat the grill to medium heat.
4. Grill wings for 8-10 mins per side until glossy and caramelized.
5. Brush with extra glaze before serving.

Tip: Garnish with sesame seeds and sliced green onions.

Nutrition Info: Calories: 240 | Fat: 9g | Carbs: 20g | Protein: 24g

Prep: 10 mins | Cook: 25 mins | Serves: 4

Ingredients:

- 800g chicken thighs
- 1/4 cup soy sauce
- 2 tbsp sesame oil
- 2 tbsp honey
- 1 tsp garlic powder
- Sesame seeds for garnish

Instructions:

1. Mix soy sauce, sesame oil, honey, and garlic powder.
2. Marinate chicken thighs for 20 mins.
3. Preheat the grill to medium-high heat.
4. Grill for 12-15 mins per side until golden and juices run clear.
5. Sprinkle with sesame seeds before serving.

Tip: Serve over a bed of stir-fried vegetables for a balanced meal.

Nutrition Info: Calories: 290 | Fat: 15g | Carbs: 8g | Protein: 30g

Prep: 15 mins | Cook: 20 mins | Serves: 4

Ingredients:

- 700g chicken drumsticks
- 1/2 cup BBQ sauce
- 3 tbsp ranch dressing
- 1 tsp onion powder
- Salt and pepper to taste

Instructions:

1. Mix BBQ sauce, ranch dressing, onion powder, salt, and pepper.
2. Toss chicken drumsticks in the mixture and marinate for 15 mins.
3. Preheat the Ninja Woodfire Electric BBQ Grill & Smoker.
4. Grill for 8-10 mins per side until caramelized and cooked through.
5. Brush with extra sauce before serving.

Tip: Serve with carrot and celery sticks for a classic combo.

Nutrition Info: Calories: 270 | Fat: 12g | Carbs: 18g | Protein: 24g

Pineapple Chili Lime Chicken

Prep: 20 mins | Cook: 15 mins | Serves: 4

Ingredients:

- 600g chicken breast, sliced
- 1 cup pineapple juice
- 2 tbsp chili powder
- 1 tbsp lime zest
- 2 tbsp olive oil
- Salt and pepper to taste

Instructions:

1. Mix pineapple juice, chili powder, lime zest, olive oil, salt, and pepper.
2. Marinate chicken slices for 30 mins.
3. Preheat the grill to medium-high heat.
4. Grill for 7-8 mins per side until pineapple-chili glaze forms.
5. Garnish with fresh cilantro before serving.

Tip: Serve over rice for a tropical twist.

Nutrition Info: Calories: 250 | Fat: 8g | Carbs: 14g | Protein: 28g

Chipotle Lime Grilled Chicken

Prep: 15 mins | Cook: 20 mins | Serves: 4

Ingredients:

- 700g chicken thighs
- 2 tbsp chipotle peppers in adobo sauce, minced
- 3 tbsp lime juice
- 2 tbsp olive oil
- 1 tsp ground cumin
- Salt and pepper to taste

Instructions:

1. Mix chipotle peppers, lime juice, olive oil, ground cumin, salt, and pepper.
2. Marinate chicken thighs for 20 mins.
3. Preheat the Ninja Woodfire Electric BBQ Grill & Smoker.
4. Grill for 10-12 mins per side until smoky and charred.
5. Squeeze extra lime juice before serving.

Tip: Pair with a cool avocado salsa for balance.

Nutrition Info: Calories: 280 | Fat: 15g | Carbs: 2g | Protein: 34g

Prep: 10 mins | Cook: 20 mins | Serves: 4

Ingredients:

- 600g chicken breasts
- 1/2 cup pesto sauce
- 3 tbsp balsamic vinegar
- 2 tbsp olive oil
- Salt and pepper to taste

Instructions:

1. Mix pesto sauce, balsamic vinegar, olive oil, salt, and pepper.
2. Marinate chicken breasts for 15 mins.
3. Preheat the grill to medium-high heat.
4. Grill for 10-12 mins per side until pesto forms a crispy crust.
5. Drizzle with extra balsamic before serving.

Tip: Serve with a side of roasted vegetables for a complete meal.

Nutrition Info: Calories: 260 | Fat: 14g | Carbs: 2g | Protein: 30g

CHAPTER THREE: BEGINNER-FRIENDLY

BURGERS

Classic Beef Burger

Prep: 15 mins | Cook: 15 mins | Serves: 4

Ingredients:

- 500g ground beef (1.1 lbs)
- 1 onion, finely diced
- 2 cloves garlic, minced
- 1 tsp Worcestershire sauce
- Salt and pepper, to taste
- 4 burger buns

Instructions:

1. Preheat your Ninja Woodfire Electric BBQ Grill & Smoker.
2. In a bowl, combine the ground beef, diced onion, minced garlic, Worcestershire sauce, salt, and pepper. Mix well.
3. Divide the mixture into 4 equal portions and shape them into burger patties.
4. Place the patties on the preheated grill and cook for about 6-8 minutes per side, or until they reach your desired level of doneness.
5. Toast the burger buns on the grill for 1-2 minutes.
6. Assemble your burgers by placing the patties in the buns and adding your favorite toppings.

Tips: Customize with lettuce, tomato, cheese, and condiments. Adjust cooking time for preferred doneness.

Nutritional Info: Calories: 350 | Fat: 18g | Carbs: 25g | Protein: 22g

Turkey and Cranberry Burger

Prep: 20 mins | Cook: 15 mins | Serves: 4

Ingredients:

- 500g ground turkey (1.1 lbs)
- 1/2 cup breadcrumbs
- 1 egg
- 1/4 cup cranberry sauce
- Salt and pepper, to taste
- 4 whole-grain burger buns

Instructions:

1. Preheat the Ninja Woodfire Electric BBQ Grill & Smoker.
2. In a bowl, combine ground turkey, breadcrumbs, egg, cranberry sauce, salt, and pepper. Mix until well combined.
3. Divide the mixture into 4 portions and form them into patties.
4. Grill the patties for 6-8 minutes per side or until fully cooked.
5. Toast the whole-grain buns on the grill for 1-2 minutes.
6. Assemble the burgers with your favorite toppings.

Tips: Add a slice of brie for extra richness. Serve with sweet potato fries.

Nutritional Info: Calories: 320 | Fat: 12g | Carbs: 30g | Protein: 22g

Southwest Black Bean Burger

Prep: 15 mins | Cook: 12 mins | Serves: 4

Ingredients:

- 400g canned black beans, drained and rinsed (14 oz)
- 1/2 cup breadcrumbs
- 1 red bell pepper, finely diced
- 1 tsp cumin
- 1 tsp chili powder
- Salt and pepper, to taste
- 4 whole-grain burger buns

Instructions:

1. Preheat your Ninja Woodfire Electric BBQ Grill & Smoker.
2. In a food processor, combine black beans, breadcrumbs, diced bell pepper, cumin, chili powder, salt, and pepper. Pulse until a thick mixture forms.
3. Divide and shape the mixture into 4 patties.
4. Grill the patties for 5-6 minutes per side until they develop a nice crust.
5. Toast the whole-grain buns on the grill for 1-2 minutes.
6. Assemble the burgers and add your preferred toppings.

Tips: Top with guacamole and salsa. Use a grill basket for easier flipping.

Nutritional Info: Calories: 280 | Fat: 5g | Carbs: 50g | Protein: 12g

Prep: 20 mins | Cook: 15 mins | Serves: 4

Ingredients:

- 500g ground beef (1.1 lbs)
- 8 slices bacon
- 1 cup cheddar cheese, shredded
- 1/4 cup BBQ sauce
- Salt and pepper, to taste
- 4 burger buns

Instructions:

1. Preheat the Ninja Woodfire Electric BBQ Grill & Smoker.
2. Form ground beef into 4 patties and season with salt and pepper.
3. Grill the patties for 6-8 minutes per side.
4. Meanwhile, cook the bacon until crispy.
5. In the last few minutes of grilling, top each patty with cheddar cheese and close the lid to melt.
6. Assemble the burgers with bacon and a drizzle of BBQ sauce.

Tips: Use a meat thermometer to ensure burgers are cooked to 160°F. Add fresh lettuce for crunch.

Nutritional Info: Calories: 420 | Fat: 22g | Carbs: 25g | Protein: 30g

Prep: 25 mins | Cook: 12 mins | Serves: 4

Ingredients:

- 500g ground lamb (1.1 lbs)
- 1/2 cup feta cheese, crumbled
- 1/4 cup Kalamata olives, chopped
- 1 tsp dried oregano
- Salt and pepper, to taste
- 4 ciabatta burger buns

Instructions:

1. Preheat your Ninja Woodfire Electric BBQ Grill & Smoker.
2. In a bowl, mix ground lamb, feta cheese, chopped olives, dried oregano, salt, and pepper.
3. Shape the mixture into 4 patties.
4. Grill the patties for 5-6 minutes per side, or until cooked to your liking.
5. Toast the ciabatta buns on the grill for 1-2 minutes.
6. Assemble the burgers and add a dollop of tzatziki sauce.

Tips: Serve with a Greek salad on the side. Use a meat thermometer to ensure lamb is cooked to 160°F.

Nutritional Info: Calories: 380 | Fat: 25g | Carbs: 20g | Protein: 22g

Teriyaki Pineapple Chicken Burger

Prep: 20 mins | Cook: 15 mins | Serves: 4

Ingredients:

- 500g ground chicken (1.1 lbs)
- 1/2 cup teriyaki sauce
- 1 cup pineapple, finely diced
- 1 tsp ginger, grated
- Salt and pepper, to taste
- 4 sesame seed burger buns

Instructions:

1. Preheat the Ninja Woodfire Electric BBQ Grill & Smoker.
2. Combine ground chicken, teriyaki sauce, diced pineapple, grated ginger, salt, and pepper in a bowl.
3. Form the mixture into 4 patties.
4. Grill the patties for 6-8 minutes per side, or until fully cooked.
5. Toast the sesame seed buns on the grill for 1-2 minutes.
6. Assemble the burgers with additional pineapple slices.

Tips: Brush extra teriyaki sauce while grilling for added flavor. Serve with coleslaw.

Nutritional Info: Calories: 320 | Fat: 15g | Carbs: 30g | Protein: 20g

Veggie Quinoa Burger

Prep: 25 mins | Cook: 10 mins | Serves: 4

Ingredients:

- 200g quinoa, cooked (1 cup)
- 400g canned chickpeas, drained and rinsed (14 oz)
- 1 carrot, grated
- 1 egg
- 1 tsp cumin
- Salt and pepper, to taste
- 4 whole-grain burger buns

Instructions:

1. Preheat your Ninja Woodfire Electric BBQ Grill & Smoker.
2. In a food processor, combine cooked quinoa, chickpeas, grated carrot, egg, cumin, salt, and pepper. Pulse until a thick mixture forms.
3. Divide and shape the mixture into 4 patties.
4. Grill the patties for 4-5 minutes per side until golden.
5. Toast the whole-grain buns on the grill for 1-2 minutes.
6. Assemble the burgers with lettuce and tzatziki.

Tips: Add a slice of avocado for creaminess. Use a grill basket for easy flipping.

Nutritional Info: Calories: 280 | Fat: 8g | Carbs: 40g | Protein: 12g

Prep: 20 mins | Cook: 15 mins | Serves: 4

Ingredients:

- 500g ground turkey (1.1 lbs)
- 1 cup mushrooms, finely chopped
- 1/2 cup blue cheese, crumbled
- 1 tsp thyme, dried
- Salt and pepper, to taste
- 4 whole-grain burger buns

Instructions:

1. Preheat the Ninja Woodfire Electric BBQ Grill & Smoker.
2. In a bowl, mix ground turkey, chopped mushrooms, blue cheese, dried thyme, salt, and pepper.
3. Form the mixture into 4 patties.
4. Grill the patties for 6-8 minutes per side, or until fully cooked.
5. Toast the whole-grain buns on the grill for 1-2 minutes.
6. Assemble the burgers with fresh arugula.

Tips: Grill the mushrooms separately for a smoky flavor. Add caramelized onions for sweetness.

Nutritional Info: Calories: 320 | Fat: 15g | Carbs: 25g | Protein: 22g

Jalapeño Pepper Jack Burger

Prep: 15 mins | Cook: 15 mins | Serves: 4

Ingredients:

- 500g ground beef (1.1 lbs)
- 1/2 cup pepper jack cheese, shredded
- 1 jalapeño, finely chopped
- 1 tsp cumin
- Salt and pepper, to taste
- 4 brioche burger buns

Instructions:

1. Preheat your Ninja Woodfire Electric BBQ Grill & Smoker.
2. Mix ground beef, shredded pepper jack cheese, chopped jalapeño, cumin, salt, and pepper in a bowl.
3. Form the mixture into 4 patties.
4. Grill the patties for 6-8 minutes per side, or until cooked through.
5. Toast the brioche buns on the grill for 1-2 minutes.
6. Assemble the burgers with sliced avocado.

Tips: Control spiciness by removing jalapeño seeds. Serve with a lime wedge for extra zing.

Nutritional Info: Calories: 380 | Fat: 20g | Carbs: 30g | Protein: 24g

Hawaiian Teriyaki Burger

Prep: 20 mins | Cook: 15 mins | Serves: 4

Ingredients:

- 500g ground beef (1.1 lbs)
- 1/2 cup pineapple, finely diced
- 1/4 cup teriyaki sauce
- 1 tsp garlic powder
- Salt and pepper, to taste
- 4 Hawaiian sweet burger buns

Instructions:

1. Preheat the Ninja Woodfire Electric BBQ Grill & Smoker.
2. Combine ground beef, diced pineapple, teriyaki sauce, garlic powder, salt, and pepper in a bowl.
3. Shape the mixture into 4 patties.
4. Grill the patties for 6-8 minutes per side, or until they reach your preferred doneness.
5. Toast the Hawaiian sweet buns on the grill for 1-2 minutes.
6. Assemble the burgers with lettuce and a slice of red onion.

Tips: Grill pineapple slices for a caramelized touch. Add a dash of extra teriyaki for more flavor.

Nutritional Info: Calories: 400 | Fat: 22g | Carbs: 30g | Protein: 22g

Salmon and Avocado Burger

Prep: 20 mins | Cook: 10 mins | Serves: 4

Ingredients:

- 500g salmon fillets, skinless and deboned (1.1 lbs)
- 1 avocado, mashed
- 1 lemon, juiced
- 2 tbsp dill, chopped
- Salt and pepper, to taste
- 4 multigrain burger buns

Instructions:

1. Preheat your Ninja Woodfire Electric BBQ Grill & Smoker.
2. Cut salmon into chunks and pulse in a food processor until coarsely ground.
3. In a bowl, mix ground salmon, mashed avocado, lemon juice, chopped dill, salt, and pepper.
4. Form the mixture into 4 patties.
5. Grill the salmon patties for 4-5 minutes per side, or until cooked through.
6. Toast the multigrain buns on the grill for 1-2 minutes.
7. Assemble the burgers with arugula and a dollop of Greek yogurt.

Tips: Use a grill mat to prevent sticking. Serve with a side of cucumber salad.

Nutritional Info: Calories: 350 | Fat: 18g | Carbs: 25g | Protein: 20g

Greek Feta and Olive Burger

Prep: 15 mins | Cook: 15 mins | Serves: 4

Ingredients:

- 500g ground beef (1.1 lbs)
- 1/2 cup feta cheese, crumbled
- 1/4 cup Kalamata olives, chopped
- 1 tsp dried oregano
- Salt and pepper, to taste
- 4 ciabatta burger buns

Instructions:

1. Preheat the Ninja Woodfire Electric BBQ Grill & Smoker.
2. Combine ground beef, crumbled feta, chopped olives, dried oregano, salt, and pepper in a bowl.
3. Form the mixture into 4 patties.
4. Grill the patties for 6-8 minutes per side, or until they reach your preferred level of doneness.
5. Toast the ciabatta buns on the grill for 1-2 minutes.
6. Assemble the burgers with lettuce and sliced tomatoes.

Tips: Brush the buns with olive oil for added richness. Grill the olives for a smoky flavor.

Nutritional Info: Calories: 380 | Fat: 22g | Carbs: 25g | Protein: 24g

Prep: 20 mins | Cook: 15 mins | Serves: 4

Ingredients:

- 500g ground chicken (1.1 lbs)
- 1/4 cup hot sauce
- 1/4 cup blue cheese dressing
- 1 celery stalk, finely chopped
- Salt and pepper, to taste
- 4 brioche burger buns

Instructions:

1. Preheat your Ninja Woodfire Electric BBQ Grill & Smoker.
2. In a bowl, combine ground chicken, hot sauce, blue cheese dressing, chopped celery, salt, and pepper.
3. Shape the mixture into 4 patties.
4. Grill the patties for 6-8 minutes per side, or until fully cooked.
5. Toast the brioche buns on the grill for 1-2 minutes.
6. Assemble the burgers with lettuce and additional blue cheese dressing.

Tips: Adjust hot sauce to your spice preference. Grill the celery for a smoky twist.

Nutritional Info: Calories: 320 | Fat: 15g | Carbs: 30g | Protein: 20g

Prep: 15 mins | Cook: 12 mins | Serves: 4

Ingredients:

- 4 large Portobello mushrooms
- 1/4 cup balsamic vinegar
- 2 tbsp olive oil
- 2 cloves garlic, minced
- Salt and pepper, to taste
- 4 whole-grain burger buns

Instructions:

1. Preheat the Ninja Woodfire Electric BBQ Grill & Smoker.
2. In a bowl, whisk together balsamic vinegar, olive oil, minced garlic, salt, and pepper.
3. Brush the Portobello mushrooms with the marinade.
4. Grill the mushrooms for 5-6 minutes per side, or until tender.
5. Toast the whole-grain buns on the grill for 1-2 minutes.
6. Assemble the burgers with spinach and a drizzle of extra balsamic.

Tips: Add a slice of melted Swiss cheese for creaminess. Grill extra mushrooms for a side dish.

Nutritional Info: Calories: 250 | Fat: 10g | Carbs: 35g | Protein: 8g

Prep: 20 mins | Cook: 15 mins | Serves: 4

Ingredients:

- 500g ground turkey (1.1 lbs)
- 1/4 cup pesto sauce
- 1 large tomato, sliced
- 1 ball fresh mozzarella, sliced
- Salt and pepper, to taste
- 4 ciabatta burger buns

Instructions:

1. Preheat your Ninja Woodfire Electric BBQ Grill & Smoker.
2. In a bowl, mix ground turkey and pesto sauce until well combined. Season with salt and pepper.
3. Shape the mixture into 4 patties.
4. Grill the turkey patties for 6-8 minutes per side, or until fully cooked.
5. Toast the ciabatta buns on the grill for 1-2 minutes.
6. Assemble the burgers with tomato slices and fresh mozzarella.

Tips: Grill the mozzarella briefly for a gooey texture. Serve with a side of mixed greens.

Nutritional Info: Calories: 300 | Fat: 15g | Carbs: 25g | Protein: 20g

CHAPTER FOUR: GRILLED VEGETABLES

FOR STARTERS

Balsamic Glazed Grilled Asparagus

Prep: 10 mins | Cook: 8 mins | Serves: 4

Ingredients:

- 300g asparagus spears, trimmed (10 oz)
- 2 tbsp balsamic glaze
- 1 tbsp olive oil
- Salt and pepper, to taste

Instructions:

1. Preheat your Ninja Woodfire Electric BBQ Grill & Smoker.
2. Toss asparagus with olive oil, salt, and pepper.
3. Grill for 4 minutes, turning occasionally.
4. Drizzle balsamic glaze over the asparagus and grill for an additional 4 minutes.

Tips: Garnish with shaved Parmesan. Be cautious with balsamic glaze to avoid burning.

Nutritional Info: Calories: 50 | Fat: 3g | Carbs: 5g | Protein: 2g

Prep: 12 mins | Cook: 6 mins | Serves: 4

Ingredients:

- 500g zucchini, sliced (1.1 lbs)
- 2 tbsp olive oil
- 1 lemon, juiced
- 2 cloves garlic, minced
- Salt and pepper, to taste

Instructions:

1. Preheat the Ninja Woodfire Electric BBQ Grill & Smoker.
2. Toss zucchini with olive oil, lemon juice, minced garlic, salt, and pepper.
3. Grill for 3 minutes per side, or until tender and slightly charred.

Tips: Sprinkle with fresh parsley. Use a grill basket for smaller zucchini slices.

Nutritional Info: Calories: 80 | Fat: 6g | Carbs: 7g | Protein: 2g

Cajun Spiced Grilled Corn

Prep: 15 mins | Cook: 10 mins | Serves: 4

Ingredients:

- 4 corn on the cob
- 2 tbsp olive oil
- 1 tbsp Cajun seasoning
- Salt and pepper, to taste

Instructions:

1. Preheat your Ninja Woodfire Electric BBQ Grill & Smoker.
2. Brush corn with olive oil and sprinkle with Cajun seasoning, salt, and pepper.
3. Grill for 10 minutes, turning occasionally, until kernels are tender and charred.

Tips: Serve with lime wedges. Soak corn in water before grilling for added moisture.

Nutritional Info: Calories: 150 | Fat: 8g | Carbs: 20g | Protein: 3g

Prep: 20 mins | Cook: 8 mins | Serves: 4

Ingredients:

- 2 large eggplants, sliced
- 1/4 cup teriyaki sauce
- 1 tbsp fresh ginger, grated
- 2 tbsp olive oil
- Salt and pepper, to taste

Instructions:

1. Preheat the Ninja Woodfire Electric BBQ Grill & Smoker.
2. Combine teriyaki sauce, grated ginger, and olive oil in a bowl.
3. Brush both sides of eggplant slices with the mixture and season with salt and pepper.
4. Grill for 4 minutes per side, or until tender and golden.

Tips: Garnish with chopped green onions. Ensure consistent thickness for even grilling.

Nutritional Info: Calories: 120 | Fat: 6g | Carbs: 15g | Protein: 2g

Prep: 15 mins | Cook: 10 mins | Serves: 4

Ingredients:

- 3 bell peppers (mixed colors), sliced
- 2 tbsp olive oil
- 1 tsp dried oregano
- 1/2 cup feta cheese, crumbled
- Salt and pepper, to taste

Instructions:

1. Preheat your Ninja Woodfire Electric BBQ Grill & Smoker.
2. Toss bell pepper slices with olive oil, dried oregano, salt, and pepper.
3. Grill for 5 minutes per side, or until tender.
4. Sprinkle crumbled feta over the grilled peppers before serving.

Tips: Add a squeeze of lemon juice. Use a grill mat to prevent sticking.

Nutritional Info: Calories: 90 | Fat: 7g | Carbs: 5g | Protein: 3g

Prep: 15 mins | Cook: 12 mins | Serves: 4

Ingredients:

- 500g Brussels sprouts, halved (1.1 lbs)
- 2 tbsp honey
- 1 tbsp Sriracha sauce
- 2 tbsp olive oil
- Salt and pepper, to taste

Instructions:

1. Preheat the Ninja Woodfire Electric BBQ Grill & Smoker.
2. In a bowl, mix honey, Sriracha sauce, and olive oil.
3. Toss Brussels sprouts with the honey Sriracha mixture, salt, and pepper.
4. Grill for 6 minutes per side, or until Brussels sprouts are caramelized.

Tips: Skewer Brussels sprouts for easy turning. Adjust Sriracha for desired spice level.

Nutritional Info: Calories: 120 | Fat: 7g | Carbs: 15g | Protein: 3g

Prep: 10 mins | Cook: 8 mins | Serves: 4

Ingredients:

- 500g cherry tomatoes (1.1 lbs)
- 2 tbsp olive oil
- 1/4 cup Parmesan cheese, grated
- 1 tsp dried Italian herbs
- Salt and pepper, to taste

Instructions:

1. Preheat your Ninja Woodfire Electric BBQ Grill & Smoker.
2. Toss cherry tomatoes with olive oil, grated Parmesan, dried Italian herbs, salt, and pepper.
3. Skewer the tomatoes or use a grill basket.
4. Grill for 4 minutes, turning occasionally, until tomatoes are slightly charred.

Tips: Serve with fresh basil. Use a mix of tomato colors for visual appeal.

Nutritional Info: Calories: 90 | Fat: 7g | Carbs: 5g | Protein: 3g

Prep: 20 mins | Cook: 15 mins | Serves: 4

Ingredients:

- 500g baby potatoes, halved (1.1 lbs)
- 2 tbsp olive oil
- 1 tbsp Dijon mustard
- 1 tsp fresh rosemary, chopped
- Salt and pepper, to taste

Instructions:

1. Preheat the Ninja Woodfire Electric BBQ Grill & Smoker.
2. Mix olive oil, Dijon mustard, chopped rosemary, salt, and pepper in a bowl.
3. Toss baby potatoes in the mixture and thread onto skewers.
4. Grill for 8-10 minutes per side, or until potatoes are golden and cooked through.

Tips: Parboil potatoes for faster grilling. Double skewer for stability.

Nutritional Info: Calories: 150 | Fat: 8g | Carbs: 20g | Protein: 2g

Chili Lime Grilled Broccoli

Prep: 15 mins | Cook: 10 mins | Serves: 4

Ingredients:

- 500g broccoli florets (1.1 lbs)
- 2 tbsp olive oil
- 1 tsp chili powder
- Zest and juice of 1 lime
- Salt and pepper, to taste

Instructions:

1. Preheat your Ninja Woodfire Electric BBQ Grill & Smoker.
2. Toss broccoli florets with olive oil, chili powder, lime zest, lime juice, salt, and pepper.
3. Skewer the broccoli or use a grill basket.
4. Grill for 5 minutes per side, or until broccoli is tender and slightly charred.

Tips: Add a sprinkle of cotija cheese. Cut broccoli into uniform sizes for even cooking.

Nutritional Info: Calories: 80 | Fat: 6g | Carbs: 7g | Protein: 3g

Cumin Lime Grilled Carrots

Prep: 15 mins | Cook: 12 mins | Serves: 4

Ingredients:

- 500g carrots, sliced into sticks (1.1 lbs)
- 2 tbsp olive oil
- 1 tsp ground cumin
- Zest and juice of 1 lime
- Salt and pepper, to taste

Instructions:

1. Preheat the Ninja Woodfire Electric BBQ Grill & Smoker.
2. Toss carrot sticks with olive oil, ground cumin, lime zest, lime juice, salt, and pepper.
3. Skewer the carrots or use a grill basket.
4. Grill for 6 minutes per side, or until carrots are tender and slightly charred.

Tips: Drizzle with honey before serving. Soak skewers in water to prevent burning.

Nutritional Info: Calories: 90 | Fat: 6g | Carbs: 10g | Protein: 1g

Prep: 10 mins | Cook: 8 mins | Serves: 4

Ingredients:

- 500g mushrooms, cleaned (1.1 lbs)
- 3 tbsp butter, melted
- 3 cloves garlic, minced
- 1 tbsp fresh parsley, chopped
- Salt and pepper, to taste

Instructions:

1. Preheat your Ninja Woodfire Electric BBQ Grill & Smoker.
2. Mix melted butter, minced garlic, chopped parsley, salt, and pepper in a bowl.
3. Brush mushrooms with the garlic butter mixture.
4. Skewer the mushrooms or use a grill basket.
5. Grill for 4 minutes per side, or until mushrooms are tender and juicy.

Tips: Add a squeeze of lemon juice. Use large mushrooms for easier grilling.

Nutritional Info: Calories: 110 | Fat: 10g | Carbs: 5g | Protein: 3g

Prep: 15 mins | Cook: 8 mins | Serves: 4

Ingredients:

- 300g green beans, trimmed (10 oz)
- 2 tbsp soy sauce
- 1 tbsp sesame oil
- 1 tsp sesame seeds
- Salt and pepper, to taste

Instructions:

1. Preheat the Ninja Woodfire Electric BBQ Grill & Smoker.
2. Toss green beans with soy sauce, sesame oil, sesame seeds, salt, and pepper.
3. Skewer the green beans or use a grill basket.
4. Grill for 4 minutes per side, or until green beans are crisp-tender.

Tips: Garnish with chopped green onions. Blanch green beans before grilling for faster cooking.

Nutritional Info: Calories: 60 | Fat: 4g | Carbs: 6g | Protein: 2g

Maple Glazed Sweet Potato Wedges

Prep: 20 mins | Cook: 15 mins | Serves: 4

Ingredients:

- 2 large sweet potatoes, cut into wedges
- 2 tbsp maple syrup
- 1 tbsp olive oil
- 1/2 tsp cinnamon
- Salt and pepper, to taste

Instructions:

1. Preheat your Ninja Woodfire Electric BBQ Grill & Smoker.
2. Toss sweet potato wedges with maple syrup, olive oil, cinnamon, salt, and pepper.
3. Grill for 7-8 minutes per side, or until sweet potatoes are caramelized and tender.

Tips: Sprinkle with sea salt. Soak sweet potato wedges in water before grilling for a crisp exterior.

Nutritional Info: Calories: 120 | Fat: 4g | Carbs: 20g | Protein: 1g

Prep: 15 mins | Cook: 12 mins | Serves: 4

Ingredients:

- 1 large cauliflower, cut into florets
- 2 tbsp harissa paste
- 2 tbsp olive oil
- 1 tsp ground cumin
- Salt and pepper, to taste

Instructions:

1. Preheat the Ninja Woodfire Electric BBQ Grill & Smoker.
2. Mix harissa paste, olive oil, ground cumin, salt, and pepper in a bowl.
3. Toss cauliflower florets in the harissa mixture.
4. Skewer the cauliflower or use a grill basket.
5. Grill for 6 minutes per side, or until cauliflower is golden and cooked through.

Tips: Serve with a yogurt dipping sauce. Cut cauliflower into similar-sized florets for even grilling.

Nutritional Info: Calories: 90 | Fat: 7g | Carbs: 7g | Protein: 3g

Basil Pesto Grilled Red Onions

Prep: 10 mins | Cook: 8 mins | Serves: 4

Ingredients:

- 4 red onions, sliced into rings
- 1/4 cup basil pesto
- 2 tbsp balsamic vinegar
- Salt and pepper, to taste

Instructions:

1. Preheat your Ninja Woodfire Electric BBQ Grill & Smoker.
2. Mix basil pesto and balsamic vinegar in a bowl.
3. Brush red onion rings with the pesto mixture, salt, and pepper.
4. Grill for 4 minutes per side, or until onions are tender and slightly charred.

Tips: Use a basting brush for even coverage. Grill until the edges caramelize.

Nutritional Info: Calories: 80 | Fat: 5g | Carbs: 8g | Protein: 1g

CHAPTER 5: SMOKED PORK RIBS

Memphis Style Dry Rub Ribs

Prep: 15 mins | Cook: 3 hours | Serves: 4

Ingredients:

- 1.5 kg Pork Ribs
- 50g Brown Sugar
- 30g Paprika
- 15g Garlic Powder
- 15g Onion Powder
- 10g Cayenne Pepper
- 10g Salt
- 5g Black Pepper

Instructions:

1. Preheat your Ninja Woodfire Electric BBQ Grill & Smoker to 225°C (437°F).
2. In a bowl, mix brown sugar, paprika, garlic powder, onion powder, cayenne pepper, salt, and black pepper to create the dry rub.
3. Rub the mixture generously over the pork ribs, ensuring an even coating.
4. Place the ribs on the grill and smoke for 3 hours or until the internal temperature reaches 90°C (194°F).
5. Let the ribs rest for 10 minutes before slicing.

Tips: For an extra kick, sprinkle more cayenne pepper in the dry rub. Adjust spice levels to your liking.

Nutritional Info: Calories: 350 | Fat: 18g | Carbs: 12g | Protein: 35g

Apple Cider Glazed Baby Back Ribs

Prep: 20 mins | Cook: 2.5 hours | Serves: 4

Ingredients:

- 1.2 kg Baby Back Ribs
- 250ml Apple Cider
- 75g Brown Sugar
- 50ml Apple Cider Vinegar
- 30ml Worcestershire Sauce
- 15g Dijon Mustard
- Salt and Pepper to taste

Instructions:

1. Preheat your Ninja Woodfire Electric BBQ Grill & Smoker to 200°C (392°F).
2. Mix apple cider, brown sugar, apple cider vinegar, Worcestershire sauce, Dijon mustard, salt, and pepper in a saucepan. Simmer until it thickens.
3. Rub the ribs with salt and pepper, then place them on the grill.
4. Smoke for 2.5 hours, basting with the apple cider glaze every 30 minutes.
5. Allow the ribs to rest for 15 minutes before serving.

Tips: Brush additional glaze before serving for an extra burst of flavor.

Nutritional Info: Calories: 300 | Fat: 15g | Carbs: 20g | Protein: 25g

Prep: 15 mins | Cook: 3.5 hours | Serves: 4

Ingredients:

- 1.8 kg Spare Ribs
- 100g Brown Sugar
- 60ml Bourbon
- 45ml Soy Sauce
- 30ml Dijon Mustard
- 15ml Worcestershire Sauce
- 10g Garlic Powder
- Salt and Pepper to taste

Instructions:

1. Heat your Ninja Woodfire Electric BBQ Grill & Smoker to 220°C (428°F).
2. In a bowl, mix brown sugar, bourbon, soy sauce, Dijon mustard, Worcestershire sauce, garlic powder, salt, and pepper to create the marinade.
3. Rub the spare ribs with the marinade and let them sit for 10 minutes.
4. Place ribs on the grill and smoke for 3.5 hours or until the internal temperature reaches 93°C (199°F).
5. Slice and enjoy!

Tips: Marinate the ribs overnight for an even richer flavor.

Nutritional Info: Calories: 380 | Fat: 22g | Carbs: 18g | Protein: 30g

Cherry Cola Braised Spare Ribs

Prep: 20 mins | Cook: 3 hours | Serves: 4

Ingredients:

- 1.6 kg Spare Ribs
- 500ml Cherry Cola
- 75g Brown Sugar
- 30ml Soy Sauce
- 15ml Dijon Mustard
- 10ml Worcestershire Sauce
- 1 Cinnamon Stick
- Salt and Pepper to taste

Instructions:

1. Preheat your Ninja Woodfire Electric BBQ Grill & Smoker to 210°C (410°F).
2. Combine cherry cola, brown sugar, soy sauce, Dijon mustard, Worcestershire sauce, cinnamon stick, salt, and pepper in a saucepan. Simmer until sugar dissolves.
3. Rub spare ribs with salt and pepper, then place them on the grill.
4. Smoke for 3 hours, basting occasionally with the cherry cola mixture.
5. Allow ribs to rest for 15 minutes before slicing.

Tips: Use a cherry cola with real sugar for an authentic taste.

Nutritional Info: Calories: 360 | Fat: 20g | Carbs: 25g | Protein: 28g

Coffee Ancho Chili Rubbed Ribs

Prep: 15 mins | Cook: 3 hours | Serves: 4

Ingredients:

- 1.7 kg Pork Ribs
- 30g Coffee Grounds
- 20g Ancho Chili Powder
- 15g Brown Sugar
- 10g Smoked Paprika
- 5g Cumin
- 5g Garlic Powder
- Salt and Pepper to taste

Instructions:

1. Heat your Ninja Woodfire Electric BBQ Grill & Smoker to 225°C (437°F).
2. Mix coffee grounds, ancho chili powder, brown sugar, smoked paprika, cumin, garlic powder, salt, and pepper to create the rub.
3. Generously coat pork ribs with the rub and let them sit for 10 minutes.
4. Place ribs on the grill and smoke for 3 hours or until internal temperature reaches 90°C (194°F).
5. Rest the ribs for 10 minutes before serving.

Tips: Experiment with different coffee blends for varied flavors.

Nutritional Info: Calories: 330 | Fat: 16g | Carbs: 14g | Protein: 32g

Prep: 20 mins | Cook: 3.5 hours | Serves: 4

Ingredients:

- 1.9 kg St. Louis Ribs
- 100ml Honey
- 30ml Dijon Mustard
- 15ml Apple Cider Vinegar
- 10ml Worcestershire Sauce
- 5g Onion Powder
- 5g Garlic Powder
- Salt and Pepper to taste

Instructions:

1. Preheat your Ninja Woodfire Electric BBQ Grill & Smoker to 220°C (428°F).
2. In a bowl, mix honey, Dijon mustard, apple cider vinegar, Worcestershire sauce, onion powder, garlic powder, salt, and pepper.
3. Brush the St. Louis ribs with the honey mustard mixture, ensuring an even coating.
4. Smoke the ribs for 3.5 hours or until the internal temperature reaches 92°C (198°F).
5. Let the ribs rest for 15 minutes before slicing.

Tips: Adjust honey for desired sweetness level.

Nutritional Info: Calories: 400 | Fat: 24g | Carbs: 22g | Protein: 29g

Prep: 25 mins | Cook: 3 hours | Serves: 4

Ingredients:

- 1.5 kg Country Ribs
- 2 Peaches, mashed
- 30ml Chipotle in Adobo Sauce
- 30ml Olive Oil
- 15ml Balsamic Vinegar
- 10g Smoked Paprika
- 5g Cinnamon
- Salt and Pepper to taste

Instructions:

1. Heat your Ninja Woodfire Electric BBQ Grill & Smoker to 210°C (410°F).
2. In a blender, combine mashed peaches, chipotle in adobo sauce, olive oil, balsamic vinegar, smoked paprika, cinnamon, salt, and pepper.
3. Marinate country ribs in the peach chipotle mixture for 15 minutes.
4. Smoke ribs for 3 hours, basting occasionally with the marinade.
5. Let the ribs rest for 10 minutes before serving.

Tips: Add a pinch of cayenne for extra heat.

Nutritional Info: Calories: 320 | Fat: 18g | Carbs: 14g | Protein: 28g

Pineapple Jalapeño Glazed Ribs

Prep: 15 mins | Cook: 3.5 hours | Serves: 4

Ingredients:

- 1.8 kg Pork Ribs
- 250ml Pineapple Juice
- 2 Jalapeños, minced
- 75g Brown Sugar
- 30ml Soy Sauce
- 15ml Ginger, grated
- 5g Garlic Powder
- Salt and Pepper to taste

Instructions:

1. Preheat your Ninja Woodfire Electric BBQ Grill & Smoker to 220°C (428°F).
2. Mix pineapple juice, minced jalapeños, brown sugar, soy sauce, grated ginger, garlic powder, salt, and pepper in a bowl.
3. Brush the pork ribs with the pineapple jalapeño glaze.
4. Smoke for 3.5 hours or until the internal temperature reaches 93°C (199°F).
5. Rest the ribs for 15 minutes before slicing.

Tips: Adjust jalapeños for spice preference.

Nutritional Info: Calories: 360 | Fat: 20g | Carbs: 22g | Protein: 26g

Prep: 20 mins | Cook: 4 hours | Serves: 4

Ingredients:

- 1.2 kg Short Ribs
- 500ml Guinness Beer
- 2 Onions, sliced
- 3 Garlic Cloves, minced
- 30ml Tomato Paste
- 15ml Soy Sauce
- 10g Brown Sugar
- Salt and Pepper to taste

Instructions:

1. Heat your Ninja Woodfire Electric BBQ Grill & Smoker to 200°C (392°F).
2. Sear short ribs on the grill until browned.
3. In a Dutch oven, combine Guinness beer, sliced onions, minced garlic, tomato paste, soy sauce, brown sugar, salt, and pepper.
4. Place seared ribs in the Dutch oven and braise on the grill for 4 hours.
5. Serve short ribs with the braising liquid.

Tips: Use a dark beer for a rich flavor.

Nutritional Info: Calories: 420 | Fat: 28g | Carbs: 10g | Protein: 32g

Prep: 25 mins | Cook: 3 hours | Serves: 4

Ingredients:

- 1.5 kg Pork Belly
- 75ml Maple Syrup
- 60ml Bourbon
- 30ml Soy Sauce
- 15ml Dijon Mustard
- 10g Smoked Paprika
- 5g Black Pepper
- Salt to taste

Instructions:

1. Preheat your Ninja Woodfire Electric BBQ Grill & Smoker to 225°C (437°F).
2. Mix maple syrup, bourbon, soy sauce, Dijon mustard, smoked paprika, black pepper, and salt in a bowl.
3. Score the skin of the pork belly and rub with the maple bourbon mixture.
4. Smoke for 3 hours or until internal temperature reaches 85°C (185°F).
5. Rest the pork belly for 15 minutes before slicing.

Tips: Score the skin to enhance the flavor.

Nutritional Info: Calories: 380 | Fat: 24g | Carbs: 15g | Protein: 28g

Prep: 15 mins | Cook: 3 hours | Serves: 4

Ingredients:

- 1.7 kg Pork Ribs
- 30ml Hoisin Sauce
- 30ml Soy Sauce
- 15ml Honey
- 10ml Rice Vinegar
- 5g Chinese Five Spice
- 5g Garlic Powder
- Salt and Pepper to taste

Instructions:

1. Heat your Ninja Woodfire Electric BBQ Grill & Smoker to 220°C (428°F).
2. In a bowl, combine hoisin sauce, soy sauce, honey, rice vinegar, Chinese five spice, garlic powder, salt, and pepper.
3. Brush the pork ribs with the Asian five spice glaze.
4. Smoke for 3 hours or until internal temperature reaches 90°C (194°F).
5. Allow the ribs to rest for 10 minutes before slicing.

Tips: Sprinkle sesame seeds for an extra crunch.

Nutritional Info: Calories: 340 | Fat: 18g | Carbs: 20g | Protein: 28g

Prep: 20 mins | Cook: 2.5 hours | Serves: 4

Ingredients:

- 1 kg Rib Tips
- 150g Fresh Raspberries
- 30ml Chipotle in Adobo Sauce
- 30ml Red Wine Vinegar
- 15ml Olive Oil
- 10g Brown Sugar
- 5g Cumin
- Salt and Pepper to taste

Instructions:

1. Preheat your Ninja Woodfire Electric BBQ Grill & Smoker to 200°C (392°F).
2. Blend raspberries, chipotle in adobo sauce, red wine vinegar, olive oil, brown sugar, cumin, salt, and pepper.
3. Coat rib tips with the raspberry chipotle mixture.
4. Smoke for 2.5 hours, basting occasionally with the marinade.
5. Rest the rib tips for 15 minutes before serving.

Tips: Use frozen raspberries if fresh ones aren't available.

Nutritional Info: Calories: 280 | Fat: 15g | Carbs: 18g | Protein: 22g

Prep: 15 mins | Cook: 2 hours | Serves: 4

Ingredients:

- 1.2 kg Pork Loin
- 60g Dijon Mustard
- 30ml Olive Oil
- 15g Fresh Thyme, chopped
- 15g Fresh Rosemary, chopped
- 5g Garlic Powder
- Salt and Pepper to taste

Instructions:

1. Heat your Ninja Woodfire Electric BBQ Grill & Smoker to 210°C (410°F).
2. Mix Dijon mustard, olive oil, chopped thyme, chopped rosemary, garlic powder, salt, and pepper.
3. Rub the pork loin with the mustard and herb mixture.
4. Smoke for 2 hours or until internal temperature reaches 70°C (158°F).
5. Let the pork loin rest for 15 minutes before slicing.

Tips: Use a meat thermometer to ensure proper doneness.

Nutritional Info: Calories: 290 | Fat: 14g | Carbs: 5g | Protein: 35g

Apricot Habanero Glazed Pork Chops

Prep: 20 mins | Cook: 1.5 hours | Serves: 4

Ingredients:

- 4 Pork Chops
- 150g Apricot Preserves
- 2 Habanero Peppers, minced
- 30ml Apple Cider Vinegar
- 15ml Soy Sauce
- 10g Dried Thyme
- Salt and Pepper to taste

Instructions:

1. Preheat your Ninja Woodfire Electric BBQ Grill & Smoker to 220°C (428°F).
2. In a saucepan, combine apricot preserves, minced habanero peppers, apple cider vinegar, soy sauce, dried thyme, salt, and pepper.
3. Grill pork chops until browned, then brush with the apricot habanero glaze.
4. Smoke for 1.5 hours, basting occasionally.
5. Allow pork chops to rest for 10 minutes before serving.

Tips: Remove seeds from habanero peppers for less heat.

Nutritional Info: Calories: 310 | Fat: 15g | Carbs: 25g | Protein: 24g

Prep: 25 mins | Cook: 1.5 hours | Serves: 4

Ingredients:

- 16 Jalapeños, halved and seeds removed
- 200g Cream Cheese
- 8 Sausages, halved
- 16 Bacon Strips
- 10g Smoked Paprika
- Salt and Pepper to taste

Instructions:

1. Heat your Ninja Woodfire Electric BBQ Grill & Smoker to 200°C (392°F).
2. Stuff jalapeño halves with cream cheese.
3. Wrap each jalapeño with a halved sausage, then wrap with a bacon strip.
4. Secure with toothpicks, sprinkle with smoked paprika, salt, and pepper.
5. Smoke for 1.5 hours or until bacon is crispy.

Tips: Soak toothpicks in water for 30 minutes before using to prevent burning.

Nutritional Info: Calories: 280 | Fat: 22g | Carbs: 5g | Protein: 18g

CHAPTER FIVE: SMOKED SALMON

Brown Sugar and Dill Smoked Salmon

Prep: 15 mins | Cook: 2.5 hours | Serves: 4

Ingredients:

- 500g salmon fillet
- 50g brown sugar
- 15g dill, chopped
- 10g sea salt
- 5g black pepper

Instructions:

1. Preheat your Ninja Woodfire Electric BBQ Grill & Smoker to 225°F (107°C).
2. Mix brown sugar, dill, sea salt, and black pepper in a bowl to create the rub.
3. Pat the salmon dry and generously coat it with the rub.
4. Place the salmon on the grill grates and smoke for 2.5 hours, or until it reaches an internal temperature of 145°F (63°C).
5. Rest the smoked salmon for 10 minutes before slicing.
6. Serve and enjoy!

Tips: Soak wood chips for 30 minutes before smoking for a richer flavor.

Nutrition Info: Calories: 220 | Fat: 12g | Carbs: 10g | Protein: 22g

Prep: 20 mins | Cook: 3 hours | Serves: 4

Ingredients:

- 600g salmon fillet
- 80g maple syrup
- Zest of 1 orange
- Zest of 1 lemon
- 10g sea salt
- 5g black pepper

Instructions:

1. Preheat your Ninja Woodfire Electric BBQ Grill & Smoker to 225°F (107°C).
2. Mix maple syrup, orange zest, lemon zest, sea salt, and black pepper in a bowl.
3. Brush the salmon with the glaze mixture.
4. Smoke the salmon for 3 hours, occasionally basting with the glaze.
5. Let it rest for 10 minutes before serving.

Tips: Use a grilling mat for easy cleanup.

Nutrition Info: Calories: 250 | Fat: 14g | Carbs: 15g | Protein: 20g

Prep: 15 mins | Cook: 2.5 hours | Serves: 4

Ingredients:

- 500g salmon fillet
- 60g unsalted butter, melted
- 3 cloves garlic, minced
- 15g fresh parsley, chopped
- 10g dried thyme
- 5g sea salt

Instructions:

1. Preheat your Ninja Woodfire Electric BBQ Grill & Smoker to 225°F (107°C).
2. In a bowl, mix melted butter, minced garlic, chopped parsley, dried thyme, and sea salt.
3. Brush the salmon with the herb butter mixture.
4. Smoke for 2.5 hours or until the salmon flakes easily.
5. Let it rest for 10 minutes before slicing.

Tips: Use a cedar plank for added smokiness.

Nutrition Info: Calories: 280 | Fat: 18g | Carbs: 1g | Protein: 25g

Honey Mustard Bourbon Smoked Salmon

Prep: 20 mins | Cook: 3 hours | Serves: 4

Ingredients:

- 600g salmon fillet
- 80g honey mustard
- 60ml bourbon
- 15g brown sugar
- 5g smoked paprika
- 5g black pepper

Instructions:

1. Preheat your Ninja Woodfire Electric BBQ Grill & Smoker to 225°F (107°C).
2. Mix honey mustard, bourbon, brown sugar, smoked paprika, and black pepper in a bowl.
3. Brush the salmon with the bourbon glaze.
4. Smoke for 3 hours, basting every 30 minutes.
5. Let it rest for 10 minutes before serving.

Tips: Use a fruitwood blend for a sweet smoky flavor.

Nutrition Info: Calories: 260 | Fat: 15g | Carbs: 12g | Protein: 23g

Teriyaki Pineapple Smoked Salmon

Prep: 15 mins | Cook: 2.5 hours | Serves: 4

Ingredients:

- 500g salmon fillet
- 80ml teriyaki sauce
- 60g pineapple juice
- 30g brown sugar
- 10g grated ginger
- 5g sesame seeds

Instructions:

1. Preheat your Ninja Woodfire Electric BBQ Grill & Smoker to 225°F (107°C).
2. Mix teriyaki sauce, pineapple juice, brown sugar, grated ginger, and sesame seeds.
3. Marinate the salmon in the teriyaki mixture for 10 minutes.
4. Smoke for 2.5 hours, brushing with marinade every 30 minutes.
5. Rest for 10 minutes before slicing.

Tips: Use a fish basket for easy flipping.

Nutrition Info: Calories: 230 | Fat: 11g | Carbs: 15g | Protein: 20g

Prep: 15 mins | Cook: 2.5 hours | Serves: 4

Ingredients:

- 500g salmon fillet
- Zest of 2 lemons
- 30ml lemon juice
- 15g black pepper
- 10g garlic powder
- 5g sea salt

Instructions:

1. Preheat your Ninja Woodfire Electric BBQ Grill & Smoker to 225°F (107°C).
2. Mix lemon zest, lemon juice, black pepper, garlic powder, and sea salt.
3. Rub the salmon with the lemon pepper mixture.
4. Smoke for 2.5 hours or until the internal temperature reaches 145°F (63°C).
5. Allow it to rest for 10 minutes before serving.

Tips: Use a fish spatula for easy transfer.

Nutrition Info: Calories: 240 | Fat: 13g | Carbs: 2g | Protein: 26g

Prep: 20 mins | Cook: 3 hours | Serves: 4

Ingredients:

- 600g salmon fillet
- 60ml sriracha sauce
- Zest of 2 limes
- 30g honey
- 10g soy sauce
- 5g cilantro, chopped

Instructions:

1. Preheat your Ninja Woodfire Electric BBQ Grill & Smoker to 225°F (107°C).
2. Mix sriracha sauce, lime zest, honey, soy sauce, and chopped cilantro.
3. Glaze the salmon with the mixture.
4. Smoke for 3 hours, basting with the glaze every 30 minutes.
5. Rest for 10 minutes before slicing.

Tips: Use a smoke box for easy wood chip placement.

Nutrition Info: Calories: 270 | Fat: 14g | Carbs: 15g | Protein: 24g

Maple Cider Smoked Salmon

Prep: 15 mins | Cook: 2.5 hours | Serves: 4

Ingredients:

- 500g salmon fillet
- 80ml apple cider
- 60ml maple syrup
- 15g whole grain mustard
- 10g smoked sea salt
- 5g black pepper

Instructions:

1. Preheat your Ninja Woodfire Electric BBQ Grill & Smoker to 225°F (107°C).
2. Mix apple cider, maple syrup, whole grain mustard, smoked sea salt, and black pepper.
3. Brush the salmon with the maple cider mixture.
4. Smoke for 2.5 hours, occasionally basting.
5. Allow it to rest for 10 minutes before slicing.

Tips: Use applewood chips for a fruity aroma.

Nutrition Info: Calories: 250 | Fat: 15g | Carbs: 18g | Protein: 22g

Prep: 20 mins | Cook: 3 hours | Serves: 4

Ingredients:

- 600g salmon fillet
- 60ml bourbon
- Juice of 2 oranges
- 30g brown sugar
- 10g thyme, chopped
- 5g black pepper

Instructions:

1. Preheat your Ninja Woodfire Electric BBQ Grill & Smoker to 225°F (107°C).
2. Mix bourbon, orange juice, brown sugar, chopped thyme, and black pepper.
3. Glaze the salmon with the mixture.
4. Smoke for 3 hours, basting every 30 minutes.
5. Rest for 10 minutes before slicing.

Tips: Use a digital meat thermometer for accuracy.

Nutrition Info: Calories: 260 | Fat: 14g | Carbs: 12g | Protein: 23g

Prep: 15 mins | Cook: 2.5 hours | Serves: 4

Ingredients:

- 500g salmon fillet
- 30ml olive oil
- 15g fresh rosemary, chopped
- 10g fresh oregano, chopped
- 5g lemon zest
- 5g sea salt

Instructions:

1. Preheat your Ninja Woodfire Electric BBQ Grill & Smoker to 225°F (107°C).
2. Mix olive oil, chopped rosemary, chopped oregano, lemon zest, and sea salt.
3. Rub the salmon with the Mediterranean herb mixture.
4. Smoke for 2.5 hours or until the internal temperature reaches 145°F (63°C).
5. Rest for 10 minutes before serving.

Tips: Use a grill brush to clean the grates before smoking.

Nutrition Info: Calories: 230 | Fat: 14g | Carbs: 1g | Protein: 24g

Prep: 20 mins | Cook: 3 hours | Serves: 4

Ingredients:

- 600g salmon fillet
- 60g raspberry jam
- 30ml balsamic vinegar
- 15g Dijon mustard
- 10g brown sugar
- 5g black pepper

Instructions:

1. Preheat your Ninja Woodfire Electric BBQ Grill & Smoker to 225°F (107°C).
2. Mix raspberry jam, balsamic vinegar, Dijon mustard, brown sugar, and black pepper.
3. Glaze the salmon with the mixture.
4. Smoke for 3 hours, basting every 30 minutes.
5. Allow it to rest for 10 minutes before slicing.

Tips: Add soaked fruitwood chips for enhanced flavor.

Nutrition Info: Calories: 270 | Fat: 15g | Carbs: 20g | Protein: 23g

Prep: 15 mins | Cook: 2.5 hours | Serves: 4

Ingredients:

- 500g salmon fillet
- 60g pesto
- 30g pine nuts, crushed
- 15g Parmesan cheese, grated
- 5g sea salt
- 5g black pepper

Instructions:

1. Preheat your Ninja Woodfire Electric BBQ Grill & Smoker to 225°F (107°C).
2. Mix pesto, crushed pine nuts, grated Parmesan, sea salt, and black pepper.
3. Coat the salmon with the pesto and pine nut mixture.
4. Smoke for 2.5 hours or until the internal temperature reaches 145°F (63°C).
5. Rest for 10 minutes before serving.

Tips: Use a fish spatula for delicate flipping.

Nutrition Info: Calories: 240 | Fat: 14g | Carbs: 2g | Protein: 26g

Sesame Soy Ginger Smoked Salmon

Prep: 20 mins | Cook: 3 hours | Serves: 4

Ingredients:

- 600g salmon fillet
- 30ml soy sauce
- 20g sesame oil
- 15g fresh ginger, grated
- 10g brown sugar
- 5g sesame seeds

Instructions:

1. Preheat your Ninja Woodfire Electric BBQ Grill & Smoker to 225°F (107°C).
2. Mix soy sauce, sesame oil, grated ginger, brown sugar, and sesame seeds.
3. Marinate the salmon in the soy ginger mixture for 10 minutes.
4. Smoke for 3 hours, brushing with marinade every 30 minutes.
5. Allow it to rest for 10 minutes before slicing.

Tips: Use a fish basket for easy flipping.

Nutrition Info: Calories: 280 | Fat: 18g | Carbs: 5g | Protein: 24g

Coconut Curry Smoked Salmon

Prep: 15 mins | Cook: 2.5 hours | Serves: 4

Ingredients:

- 500g salmon fillet
- 60ml coconut milk
- 30g red curry paste
- 15g brown sugar
- 10g lime juice
- 5g cilantro, chopped

Instructions:

1. Preheat your Ninja Woodfire Electric BBQ Grill & Smoker to 225°F (107°C).
2. Mix coconut milk, red curry paste, brown sugar, lime juice, and chopped cilantro.
3. Coat the salmon with the coconut curry mixture.
4. Smoke for 2.5 hours or until the internal temperature reaches 145°F (63°C).
5. Rest for 10 minutes before serving.

Tips: Use a grilling mat for easy cleanup.

Nutrition Info: Calories: 250 | Fat: 14g | Carbs: 6g | Protein: 25g

Prep: 20 mins | Cook: 3 hours | Serves: 4

Ingredients:

- 600g salmon fillet
- 20g Cajun seasoning
- 15g paprika
- 10g onion powder
- 5g garlic powder
- 5g cayenne pepper

Instructions:

1. Preheat your Ninja Woodfire Electric BBQ Grill & Smoker to 225°F (107°C).
2. Mix Cajun seasoning, paprika, onion powder, garlic powder, and cayenne pepper.
3. Rub the salmon with the blackening spice mixture.
4. Smoke for 3 hours or until the internal temperature reaches 145°F (63°C).
5. Rest for 10 minutes before serving.

Tips: Adjust cayenne pepper to your spice preference.

Nutrition Info: Calories: 260 | Fat: 15g | Carbs: 2g | Protein: 27g

CHAPTER SIX: FLAVORFUL SMOKED

VEGETABLES

Smoked Caprese Stuffed Portobello Mushrooms

Prep: 15 mins | Cook: 30 mins | Serves: 4

Ingredients:

- 4 large Portobello mushrooms
- 200g fresh mozzarella, diced (7 oz)
- 250g cherry tomatoes, halved (9 oz)
- 1/4 cup fresh basil, chopped
- 2 tbsp balsamic glaze
- Salt and pepper to taste

Instructions:

1. Preheat your Ninja Woodfire Electric BBQ Grill & Smoker to 180°C (350°F).
2. Clean Portobello mushrooms and remove stems.
3. In a bowl, mix mozzarella, cherry tomatoes, basil, salt, and pepper.
4. Stuff each mushroom with the mixture.
5. Place mushrooms on the grill grates and smoke for 30 minutes.
6. Drizzle balsamic glaze over the mushrooms before serving.

Tips: Add a touch of olive oil to enhance the flavors. Serve as a delightful side or main dish.

Nutrition Info: Calories: 180 | Fat: 8g | Carbs: 12g | Protein: 15g

Mesquite Smoked Spaghetti Squash

Prep: 10 mins | Cook: 1 hour | Serves: 4

Ingredients:

- 1 medium spaghetti squash (about 1.5 kg)
- 2 tbsp olive oil
- 2 tsp mesquite seasoning
- Salt and pepper to taste
- Fresh parsley for garnish

Instructions:

1. Cut spaghetti squash in half lengthwise and scoop out seeds.
2. Brush each half with olive oil, then season with mesquite, salt, and pepper.
3. Preheat the grill to 200°C (400°F).
4. Place the squash halves on the grill, cut side down, and smoke for 1 hour.
5. Scrape the squash with a fork to create "noodles."
6. Garnish with fresh parsley before serving.

Tips: Customize with your favorite herbs. Serve as a low-carb alternative to pasta.

Nutrition Info: Calories: 120 | Fat: 7g | Carbs: 15g | Protein: 2g

Prep: 15 mins | Cook: 30 mins | Serves: 6

Ingredients:

- 500g Brussels sprouts, halved (1.1 lb)
- 3 tbsp olive oil
- 2 tsp applewood seasoning
- Salt and pepper to taste
- 2 tbsp balsamic vinegar

Instructions:

1. Trim and halve Brussels sprouts.
2. Toss with olive oil, applewood seasoning, salt, and pepper.
3. Preheat the grill to 200°C (400°F).
4. Place Brussels sprouts on a grill pan and smoke for 30 minutes.
5. Drizzle balsamic vinegar over the sprouts before serving.

Tips: Add a sprinkle of Parmesan for extra flavor. Perfect as a side for any BBQ dish.

Nutrition Info: Calories: 90 | Fat: 6g | Carbs: 8g | Protein: 3g

Prep: 20 mins | Cook: 45 mins | Serves: 4

Ingredients:

- 4 large bell peppers, halved and seeds removed
- 250g ground beef (9 oz)
- 1 cup cooked quinoa
- 1 cup black beans, drained and rinsed
- 1 cup diced tomatoes
- 1 tsp hickory seasoning
- Salt and pepper to taste
- 1 cup shredded cheddar cheese

Instructions:

1. Preheat the Ninja Woodfire Electric BBQ Grill & Smoker to 180°C (350°F).
2. In a skillet, brown ground beef and season with hickory, salt, and pepper.
3. In a bowl, mix cooked beef, quinoa, black beans, tomatoes, and cheese.
4. Stuff each bell pepper half with the mixture.
5. Place peppers on the grill grates and smoke for 45 minutes.

Tips: Customize with your preferred protein. Top with sour cream before serving.

Nutrition Info: Calories: 320 | Fat: 15g | Carbs: 30g | Protein: 18g

Prep: 15 mins | Cook: 25 mins | Serves: 4

Ingredients:

- 1 large cauliflower
- 3 tbsp olive oil
- 4 cloves garlic, minced
- 1 tsp dried herbs (rosemary, thyme, oregano)
- Salt and pepper to taste
- Lemon wedges for serving

Instructions:

1. Slice cauliflower into 1-inch steaks.
2. In a bowl, mix olive oil, minced garlic, dried herbs, salt, and pepper.
3. Preheat the grill to 200°C (400°F).
4. Brush cauliflower steaks with the herb mixture.
5. Smoke on the grill for 25 minutes or until tender.
6. Serve with a squeeze of fresh lemon.

Tips: Add a sprinkle of Parmesan for extra richness. Great as a meat-free main.

Nutrition Info: Calories: 120 | Fat: 8g | Carbs: 12g | Protein: 4g

Prep: 10 mins | Cook: 20 mins | Serves: 4

Ingredients:

- 4 corn on the cob, husked
- 4 tbsp butter, melted
- 1 tsp cherrywood seasoning
- Salt to taste
- Fresh cilantro for garnish

Instructions:

1. Brush corn with melted butter, then season with cherrywood and salt.
2. Preheat the Ninja Woodfire Electric BBQ Grill & Smoker to 180°C (350°F).
3. Place corn on the grill grates and smoke for 20 minutes.
4. Rotate the corn occasionally for even cooking.
5. Garnish with fresh cilantro before serving.

Tips: Add a dash of lime juice for extra freshness. Perfect summer side dish.

Nutrition Info: Calories: 180 | Fat: 12g | Carbs: 18g | Protein: 3g

Prep: 10 mins | Cook: 15 mins | Serves: 4

Ingredients:

- 500g asparagus spears, trimmed (1.1 lb)
- 3 tbsp olive oil
- 1 tsp garlic powder
- Salt and pepper to taste
- 1/2 cup grated Parmesan cheese

Instructions:

1. Toss asparagus with olive oil, garlic powder, salt, and pepper.
2. Preheat the grill to 200°C (400°F).
3. Bundle 5-6 asparagus spears together and wrap with kitchen twine.
4. Place bundles on the grill grates and smoke for 15 minutes.
5. Sprinkle Parmesan over the bundles before serving.

Tips: Drizzle with balsamic reduction for an extra kick. Elegant side for any occasion.

Nutrition Info: Calories: 120 | Fat: 9g | Carbs: 6g | Protein: 6g

Prep: 15 mins | Cook: 30 mins | Serves: 4

Ingredients:

- 2 large sweet potatoes, peeled and sliced
- 3 tbsp olive oil
- 2 tsp pecan seasoning
- Salt and pepper to taste
- Fresh thyme for garnish

Instructions:

1. Toss sweet potato slices with olive oil, pecan seasoning, salt, and pepper.
2. Preheat the Ninja Woodfire Electric BBQ Grill & Smoker to 180°C (350°F).
3. Arrange sweet potato medallions on the grill grates and smoke for 30 minutes.
4. Garnish with fresh thyme before serving.

Tips: Add a sprinkle of cinnamon for a hint of sweetness. Perfect autumn side dish.

Nutrition Info: Calories: 150 | Fat: 8g | Carbs: 18g | Protein: 2g

Prep: 20 mins | Cook: 45 mins | Serves: 4

Ingredients:

- 1 acorn squash, sliced
- 3 tbsp maple syrup
- 1 tsp cinnamon
- Salt and pepper to taste
- Chopped pecans for garnish

Instructions:

1. In a bowl, mix acorn squash slices with maple syrup, cinnamon, salt, and pepper.
2. Preheat the grill to 200°C (400°F).
3. Place the squash slices on a cedar plank and smoke for 45 minutes.
4. Garnish with chopped pecans before serving.

Tips: Serve with a dollop of whipped cream. A delightful holiday side dish.

Nutrition Info: Calories: 180 | Fat: 6g | Carbs: 30g | Protein: 2g

Prep: 10 mins | Cook: 20 mins | Serves: 4

Ingredients:

- 1 can (400g) artichoke hearts, drained (14 oz)
- 2 tbsp olive oil
- 1 tsp mesquite seasoning
- Salt and pepper to taste
- Lemon wedges for serving

Instructions:

1. Toss artichoke hearts with olive oil, mesquite seasoning, salt, and pepper.
2. Preheat the Ninja Woodfire Electric BBQ Grill & Smoker to 180°C (350°F).
3. Place artichoke hearts on the grill grates and smoke for 20 minutes.
4. Serve with lemon wedges for a zesty touch.

Tips: Add a sprinkle of Parmesan before smoking. Great as an appetizer or side dish.

Nutrition Info: Calories: 120 | Fat: 8g | Carbs: 10g | Protein: 2g

Prep: 15 mins | Cook: 25 mins | Serves: 4

Ingredients:

- 500g broccoli florets (1.1 lb)
- 1 cup cheddar cheese, shredded
- 2 eggs, beaten
- 1/2 cup breadcrumbs
- 1 tsp alderwood seasoning
- Salt and pepper to taste
- Sour cream for dipping

Instructions:

1. Steam broccoli until tender, then chop finely.
2. In a bowl, combine broccoli, cheddar cheese, eggs, breadcrumbs, alderwood seasoning, salt, and pepper.
3. Preheat the grill to 200°C (400°F).
4. Form mixture into bite-sized balls and place on a grill-safe tray.
5. Smoke for 25 minutes or until golden brown.
6. Serve with a side of sour cream for dipping.

Tips: Add diced ham for extra flavor. A crowd-pleasing appetizer.

Nutrition Info: Calories: 180 | Fat: 10g | Carbs: 15g | Protein: 8g

Prep: 20 mins | Cook: 40 mins | Serves: 6

Ingredients:

- 1 eggplant, diced
- 2 zucchinis, sliced
- 1 red bell pepper, diced
- 1 yellow bell pepper, diced
- 1 onion, diced
- 2 cloves garlic, minced
- 3 tbsp olive oil
- 2 tsp rosemary, chopped
- Salt and pepper to taste
- 1 can (400g) diced tomatoes (14 oz)

Instructions:

1. In a large bowl, mix eggplant, zucchinis, bell peppers, onion, garlic, olive oil, rosemary, salt, and pepper.
2. Preheat the Ninja Woodfire Electric BBQ Grill & Smoker to 180°C (350°F).
3. Place the vegetable mixture in a grill-safe pan and smoke for 40 minutes.
4. Stir in diced tomatoes before serving.

Tips: Serve over rice or pasta. A hearty and healthy dish.

Nutrition Info: Calories: 150 | Fat: 8g | Carbs: 18g | Protein: 4g

Prep: 10 mins | Cook: 30 mins | Serves: 4

Ingredients:

- 500g baby carrots (1.1 lb)
- 3 tbsp maple syrup
- 2 tbsp bourbon
- 2 tbsp butter
- 1 tsp Dijon mustard
- Salt and pepper to taste
- Chopped parsley for garnish

Instructions:

1. Toss carrots with maple syrup, bourbon, melted butter, Dijon mustard, salt, and pepper.
2. Preheat the grill to 200°C (400°F).
3. Place carrots on a grill-safe tray and smoke for 30 minutes.
4. Garnish with chopped parsley before serving.

Tips: Add a pinch of cayenne for a spicy kick. A sweet and savory side.

Nutrition Info: Calories: 120 | Fat: 6g | Carbs: 18g | Protein: 1g

Prep: 15 mins | Cook: 20 mins | Serves: 4

Ingredients:

- 2 avocados, halved and pitted
- 2 tbsp olive oil
- 1 tsp chipotle seasoning
- Zest and juice of 1 lime
- Salt and pepper to taste
- Fresh cilantro for garnish

Instructions:

1. Brush avocado halves with olive oil, then season with chipotle, lime zest, lime juice, salt, and pepper.
2. Preheat the Ninja Woodfire Electric BBQ Grill & Smoker to 180°C (350°F).
3. Place avocados on the grill grates and smoke for 20 minutes.
4. Garnish with fresh cilantro before serving.

Tips: Serve over a salad or as a tasty snack. Enhance with a sprinkle of cotija cheese.

Nutrition Info: Calories: 160 | Fat: 14g | Carbs: 8g | Protein: 2g

Prep: 20 mins | Cook: 15 mins | Serves: 4

Ingredients:

- 1 cucumber, cut into chunks
- 200g cherry tomatoes (7 oz)
- 150g feta cheese, cubed (5 oz)
- 1 red onion, cut into wedges
- 1/4 cup Kalamata olives
- 2 tbsp olive oil
- 1 tsp dried oregano
- Salt and pepper to taste
- Wooden skewers, soaked in water

Instructions:

1. Thread cucumber, cherry tomatoes, feta cheese, red onion, and olives onto skewers.
2. In a bowl, mix olive oil, dried oregano, salt, and pepper.
3. Preheat the grill to 200°C (400°F).
4. Brush skewers with the olive oil mixture.
5. Grill for 15 minutes, turning occasionally, until vegetables are lightly charred.
6. Serve as a refreshing appetizer or side dish.

Tips: Customize with your favorite Greek salad ingredients. Drizzle with balsamic glaze.

Nutrition Info: Calories: 180 | Fat: 15g | Carbs: 8g | Protein: 5g

CHAPTER SEVEN: NEXT-LEVEL

TECHNIQUES FOR BACKYARD GREATNESS

You've conquered smoking, searing and basic operating protocols. Now it's time to propel your live-fire prowess to the next level with advanced mastery tips. From showstopping reverse sears to smoke-kissed whole beasts, let's max out your Ninja Woodfire Grill's potential!

The Art of the Reverse Sear

Perfectly cooked meat boasts a crisp, flavor-packed exterior yet moist, tender interior. The reverse sear delivers on both fronts by slowly roasting first and then searing at the finale.

Advantages Over Traditional Searing

Standard grilling sears meat immediately after seasoning which:

- Can over-dry & toughen exterior

- Leads to unevenly cooked interiors

Reverse searing does the opposite:

- Gently roasts meat at 250-275°F until 5-10°F under target temp

- Then blasts the exterior with 550°+ direct heat to finish

Benefits include enhanced juiciness, edge-to-edge doneness and bonus smoky essence from the prolonged cook time.

Prime Proteins for the Reverse Treatment

Thicker, fatty cuts truly shine when reverse seared including:

- Juicy Ribeyes

- Perfect Porterhouses

- Succulent Filet Mignon

- Extra-tender Prime Rib Roasts

- Bone-in Pork Chops

Divide & Conquer with Two-Zone Grilling

By configuring separate direct and indirect heat zones, the grill effectively multitasks. The direct side provides scorching heat for searing while the indirect side gently roasts.

Setting Up the Two Zones

Creating two distinct thermal environments means:

- Piling charcoal/wood on just one side

- Leaving other side empty

- Place meat needing gentler heat on empty side

- Close lid to contain heat

Cooking Applications

Typical uses for two-zone grilling include:

- Reverse searing thick steaks

- Crisping chicken skin before indirect roast

- Slow-smoking ribs low'n'slow while also searing kebobs

- Finishing larger roasts without scorching exterior

- Infusing smoky essence into sides like baked beans

The flexibility empowers you to grill various foods simultaneously despite differing cook times and temperatures.

Epic Smokes: Low'n Slow Whole Beast Mode

Your Ninja Woodfire Grill truly proves its might when tasked with mammoth cuts of meat requiring prolonged exposure to low, smoky heat before emerging tender and brimming with flavor.

Heavyweight Smoking Contenders

The following huge cuts shine when given the low'n'slow treatment:

- Beef brisket

- Pork shoulder (pulled pork)

- Beef short ribs

- Rack of lamb

- Whole turkey

- Whole chickens

- Smoked ham

Vital Strategies for Smokehouse Success

When dealing with hulking cuts, these tips lead to mouthwatering outcomes:

- Secure even 225-250°F temps across grill

- Add soaked woodchunks to integrated smoking box

- Expect 1-2 hours per lb (go by meat temp not times)

- Wrap meat at halfway mark to protect from drying

- Let rest 30-60 minutes before serving for moisture retention

The dividends of patience? Succulently tender texture with smokehouse essence in every bite!

By broadening your live-fire grilling repertoire with these advanced tricks, mundane burgers become a distant memory. Now let's get to cookin'!

Troubleshooting & Care - Keeping Your Grill in Peak Form

Even the most masterful backyard grillmasters encounter the occasional hiccup. But arming yourself with preventative care insights and troubleshooting savvy ensures your Ninja Woodfire Grill stays primed for woodfired greatness. This chapter help you nip common challenges in the bud - plus simplify maintenance so you can focus on fun instead of fussing. Let's keep that grill sizzling!

Six Sizzling Hot Troubleshooting Tips

Uneven Cooking Dilemmas Solved

The Issue: Some foods char faster than others despite equal grill time.

likely Causes:

• Inconsistent interior heat distribution

• Overcrowded grilling surface obstructing airflow

• Line of site between food and heat source gets blocked

The Fix:

1. Leave ample room between foods for proper airflow circulation.

2. Use ambient thermometer to identify cooler vs hotter zones then rearrange placement accordingly.

3. Rotate foods every 5-7 minutes especially over direct heat.

Excessive Smoke Signals

The Issue: Billowing white clouds engulf foods, overpowering flavor.

Likely Causes:

• Woodchip box overfilled

• Ventilation obstructed

• Grease flare-up

The Fix:

1. Use fewer woodchunks in smoker box.

2. Check that lid vent is fully open.

3. Foil-wrap woodschunks to reduce smoldering.

4. Clean grill regularly to prevent grease buildup.

Temperature Flux Frustrations

The Issue: Set temp readout doesn't match ambient cooking temperature.

Likely Causes:

• Thermostat calibration needed

• Airflow disruption

The Fix:

1. Manually calibrate thermostat following product instructions.

2. Reduce open/close lid frequency.

3. Use ambient thermometer to accurately track temps.

Protecting Your Investment with Preventative Care

Storage & Protection Best Practices

1. Deploy Weatherproof Cover

Investing in a heavy duty, water resistant cover protects your grill from rain, snow and dirt year-round when not cooking.

2. Store Properly During Off Season

Place wood pellets/charcoal bags in airtight containers away from moisture when grill is not in regular use to prevent mold.

3. Check/Address Small Repairs

Fix minor dings, tighten loose screws, seal small leaks early before escalating into larger headaches.

4. Clean Ash Bin Frequently

Letting ashes build up negatively impacts airflow which affects temperature regulation.

Routine Maintenance Matters

1. Thorough Cleaning Ritual

From clearing grease traps to brushing grates after each cookout, keeping your grill tidy improves performance while guarding against uncontrolled flareups.

2. Wet Climate Protection

For regions prone to high humidity/rain, apply added safeguards like weatherproof grill cover/wind guards and moisture absorbing pellets in smoker box.

3. Season Grates

Prevent food from sticking while enhancing flavor by periodically seasoning grates with non-stick vegetable spray or oil.

With preventative care and troubleshooting savvy in your back pocket, you can sidestep potential pitfalls and simply relax into the languorous world of smoking, searing or roasting up your next masterpiece. So fire it up and enjoy!

Conclusion

We've covered a lot of ground on your journey to becoming a backyard barbecue legend thanks to the trailblazing Ninja Woodfire Grill. Let's recap some of the most crucial skills and knowledge nuggets:

Proper setup - From assembly to ideal outdoor placement protocols, those vital first steps establish a solid grilling foundation. Temperature mastery - Whether calibrating control buttons or configuring direct vs indirect heat zones, understanding how to harness temperatures empowers cooking precision.

Grilling basics - From properly oiling hot grates before searing to resisting the urge to flip foods too frequently, those fundamental techniques ensure success.

Smoking essentials - Low and slow is the mantra, while wood selection and strategic setup allow for infusing foods with mouthwatering smoky richness.

Handy accessories - Quality tools like tongs, instant-read thermometers, grill brushes and more make the process smoother.

Preventative care - From cleaning grease traps to weatherproof storage covers, those acts of grill TLC boost longevity dramatically.

Encouragement for Creative Experimentation

While this guide has equipped you with a library of incredibly helpful knowledge to unlock woodfired greatness, don't be afraid to channel your inner innovative pitmaster!

Experiment with novel wood combinations in the smoker box to create your signature flavor profile. Try grilling unexpected ingredients like fruit, veggies and seafood using both direct and indirect heat. Explore the Ninja Foodi's bonus capabilities like dehydrating jerky or crafting the perfect wood-fired pizza thanks to the grill's dedicated pizza oven attachment.

The possibilities are truly endless when you marry professional-caliber equipment like the Ninja Woodfire Grill with your creative vision and lust for backyard innovation. Trust yourself, think outside the box and have fun with it! Your neighborhood will soon view you as the grillmaster to be reckoned with thanks to your trailblazing feats of live-fire brilliance.

So spark that grill and invite everyone over...the food is gonna be legendary!

Made in United States
Orlando, FL
06 May 2024

46565622R00070